A FUTURE PERFECT

A FUTURE PERFECT

POEMS

RAZIELLE AIGEN

TALONBOOKS

Talonbooks
9259 Shaughnessy Street, Vancouver, British Columbia, Canada V6P 6R4
talonbooks.com

Talonbooks is located on xʷməθkʷəy̓əm, Sḵwx̱wú7mesh, Stó:lō, and səl̓ilwətaʔɬ Lands.

First printing: 2021

Typeset in Minion
Printed and bound in Canada on 100% post-consumer recycled paper

Cover and interior design by Typesmith
Cover illustration, *Petals* by Ginger Sedlarova

Talonbooks acknowledges the financial support of the Canada Council for the Arts, the Government of Canada through the Canada Book Fund, and the Province of British Columbia through the British Columbia Arts Council and the Book Publishing Tax Credit.

Library and Archives Canada Cataloguing in Publication

Title: A future perfect : poetry / by Razielle Aigen.
Names: Aigen, Razielle, author.
Description: Includes bibliographical references.
Identifiers: Canadiana 20210199865 | ISBN 9781772013658 (softcover)
Classification: LCC PS8601.I32 F88 2021 | DDC C811/.6—dc23

for Serge

WINTERING

She's wintering
they say, mostly
because of how she cancels
herself out. Blanketing
the drifting. Time is
what is happening.
At any given cross-section
a lifetime is spanning. Tinting
at the beginning of being. A tree
growing outwards, branching horizontally
stalls its own growth.
dormancy. restoring. Resorting
to slumber. Sleep sleeping itself
through a winter of mostly.
They're saying she's growing.
beginning. stalling. Cancelling
herself out of happening.
A story. life. lifetimes.
Snowdrifts drifting
blanketing the branching.
By this they'll have meant
to say, mostly
that she is
what is happening.
A tint of timing
the being of a beginning
spanning a lifetime.
wintering. expanding.
Branching out.

MOSTLY WATER

The light changed
moving the green
that was right now
through the trees

Wanting nothing
more than to tell you the sky
was orange and that maybe
I'm more
of an idea

No words
no thought
no Greek tragedy

I'm glad we spent the evening in the park

If it's any consolation
my dear, we are mostly
water

GENE LOSS

Has it happened yet?
Have you sprouted a feather, a tail
a fin, or a gill? Has a leaf or a blade of grass pushed up
between your antlers? Have the heavyweight wisteria and
clematis vined their way around
the trellis of your shoulder blades
wrapping around the coracoid processes, latching
onto the phalanges of your wings?

Are you in bloom?
Have you started to decompose?
Have you made that lateral shift into a tangled thicket
a mutated chimerical being of light and wonder?
Are you enjoying your next life as a rabbit-toad?
Are you evolved? Have you permitted it to happen
without resistance? Has the glee of recombination taken over?

Is your incarnation underway?
Have there been any glitches?
Complications? Are you stuck in a net
meant for trout or clams? Has a trap been set?
Are you okay? Are you beside yourself, suspended in disbelief
that you are now also part fern? Do you need
a guide for the perplexed
moss on your knees as you furrow through this horizontal
transference, renegotiating a shift

in

molecules

dropping off the *y*

sliding sideways

into the *x*

axis of infinite possibility?

You are free now.
You must be so happy
finally to become the leopard-heron
you've always known yourself to be.
You're co-evolving. It's your time, you can do it.
You're a boy from Brooklyn *and* a single-celled organism
of the sea dreaming in an ocean bed.

You are becoming more you.
You are composting
decomposing, in transition
on your way back to becoming
earth, minerals enjoyed by worms.
By now your bones are probably reduced
to dust, a pulp, a fine mist. I want to help you
understand these new life forms, help you
shovel your way towards realizing
your infinite potential.

Can't you see how great it is?
You are asparagus *and* star!
Even though my gut feeling is still no
this is not okay, it's happening.
Embrace the gene loss.
I'm happy for you. Really
I am. No mother. No father. No origin.

You are overlapping realities
cross-pollinating with everything.
You are an arachnid-hydrangea
a rattlesnake-bee, a rainforest-lamppost
malleable, fluid, in flux.
You are cosmic intelligence.
You are geology.
You are changing
but the sun remains the same.
You are becoming more you.

You are now in process
giving off gasses, an ozone unto yourself.
You're the physics of a petal, the mathematics of rain
the sacred geometry of a trilobite encrusted in rock.
You've gone primal, cut loose all ties
the knots and tassels of your remembrances
clipped, committed to memory.

You know all the prayers by heart.

YOU ARE NOW MORE YOU

You are swimming away

Your skin isn't really doing the job
it's not keeping things out
and it's not keeping you in

Your pores are flooded
there are deep folds
where it used to be taut

Caught
by surprise

by the postural warp
and woof

of your stoop
hanging

in the hallway
mirror (a decoy)
a way to enlarge
a narrow
space

if only
by reflection

You are now more you than ever
You are not your face

You are not your name

AFTER YOU WENT NOVA

Tiny pinpricks
punched through a black backlit
sheet of paper. A handcrafted galaxy.

Capitulated constellations.
A Milky Way of want
starry starry grasping
at being as such.

And what if
everything we saw
everything we did
everything we said
everything we said we saw
everything we said we did
and did everything we said
we would, were congruent, aligned?

Folding even pleats
in the night sky
we become mysterious
to ourselves.
open. adaptable. origami.
Fission of impossible
proportion.

We sharpen the folds
defining our creases
with a filed whale bone
that feels good to hold.
We meet our edge.
We close our eyes.
We envision one thousand of us
taking flight. A wish
to live more
simply.

Waking we are greeted by the morning star.

When it's over
I'll have moved to Marfa, Texas
in impenetrable aloneness.

A plot of land. A tiny home.
Green beans and cherry tomatoes.
corrugated. contained. Bending
the possibility of possibility.

Seeing from the inside, together
we emerge in congruence
lighter somehow.

Who knew this being as such
would go on being
after you went nova.

By obscure means we alter each other
in a future perfect

we will have become who the other ought to have been.

A POEM ABOUT A DREAM ABOUT A MAN WHO DRANK TEA, HAD LOOSE IDEAS ABOUT GRAVITY, AND DIED TRYING TO TRANSVERSE THE SEVEN BRIDGES OF KÖNIGSBERG BY FALLING DOWN AN ELEVATOR SHAFT

I.

In a topology of open space
        recurrent dream
        measures keep time
for the movement of tea-field theories
        the intersection of subsets
        a family

Holding together non-empty
        disjointed unions
        we will have come to accept
(loose leaves) as sub-spheres
        of control, a reckoning
        that everything is more or less

connected by degrees of order and chaos, formlessness and form

II.

It doesn't really matter
        whether the edges
        are straight
or curved, or whether one
        node is a little
        to the left

Under continuous deformations
        (stretching, bending
        but not tearing)
we stuff our little faces
        in his underarm
        sniffing out

an enmeshed togetherness

III.

By way of seven bridges
he could conditionally
cross each one
no more than once, by this
all that will have been
meant was that you don't ever leave land mass

By varying degrees
of familial freedom
the trick is to
reach an island or mainland
but what will have
mattered most

in the end is the sequence, the genealogical conjecture
that what we say matters

IV.

Consider for the sake of example
        a father's love
        a bamboo forest
an underground network
        a rhizome grove
        in which moving

towards any given point
        is always the same
        distance
as moving away from
        the place
        of departure

in other words, the number of times one enters will always equal
the number of times one leaves

v.

Or, to put it more simply
        one always leaves
        and enters by
what we think of as a bridge
        criss-crossing over what we think
        of as rushing waters

A homonym like "leaves"
        is bound
        to plant
the seedlings of thought
        about seasonal
        change

brooding, a honeycomb secretes its nectar, adding sweetness
to the clouding of milk

VI.

His grid, a meticulous telegraphing
    of point A
    to point B
a baseline held down by a steady
    rhythm of return
    protector/provider

Disseminating a magnetism
    not unlike
    seven bridges
over bodies of water
    that keep us close
    to home

milk and honey added for gravity

VII.

In truth what we think
            is irrelevant
            is what lies
at the very heart of the matter
          a neighbourhood
          that we've come to

consider as the permissible distance
            to travel within
            what we call a graph or a family
because of the vertices and nodes
          their connecting edges
          is beside the point

grafted familial traces bridge the distance to another
neighbourhood of time

viii.

In reality
          it just won't matter
          that much
(an attitude adopted
          as a function
          of age)

age adding
          a dimension
          of flavour to the brew
making it more
          full-bodied
          over time

the renunciation of telos settles in as it steeps

IX.

In the manifolds formed
without self-
intersection
are where some of his best
sermons
and thoughts

will be resurrected, a retrospective
of highlights
that promise
to reflect the singular clarity
of a diamond
mind

in perennial return to the clouding of understanding

x.

Embedded as either
        a plane or
        a sphere
an illusion, always a sleight
        of hand
        giving the appearance

of being
        free
        to leave
anytime, though
        the density
        of mass

will not have allowed diversion, not the slightest figure of eight

XI.

A drift towards any other
    easily non-orientable
    loci
makes certain
    that when immersed
    in three-dimensional space

that where something is
    placed
    is always
traceable
    to a point
    of origin

a softer tracking device than most will have put a positive spin
on all possible worlds

XII.

What could he have possibly
    been thinking
    in the moments prior

to giving up his heart
    before making
    a final exit

down an elevator shaft
    a lunar eclipse
    that lasted

only a matter of seconds?
    In the advent
    of that grand finale

he offered a system
    of intuitively
    appealing axioms

applicable only if
    their gravitational
    field was weak

Otherwise providing no more
    than a good approximation
    a hope

that things stay close, that things stick
    to a surface
    that things get pulled

down to a centre
        that things
        don't go

flying away
        that things
        do not leave

A different way of saying
        this is that
        now we trust more

not what we know
        of what he thought
        but how he felt

XIII.

On the upshot
he didn't leave
fear a chance
to set in

(((((((((no consciousness)))))))))

(((((((((only incandescent oolong orbs of clear white light)))))))))

(((((((((pooling in the left and right lobes of the brain)))))))))

(((((((((hemispheres of who you are)))))))))

(((((((((a mystical aura behind his eyes)))))))))

(((((((((filled with tears of joy)))))))))

XIV.

In addendum

From where he stood
        the other side
        was visible
the whole entire world

((((((((((EVERYTHING))))))))))

in its entirety
        now
        connected
by a single narrow bridge

HELLO, WORLD!

I like the way life collects itself
around you. wind and sun.
You say, *I'm in the mood of the night*
and then it's like, *hello, world!*
when our faces touch
a touch
like the fetal zone
inside a womb
where there's room.
warm. womb-like. womb life. lifelike.

Light cast
on the dark places
where we touch
reprogramming
our basic syntax
morning moods
our faces
a resemblance
of who we might have been
before we closed our eyes.
blank spaces. world. zone. night.

Just there
in the where where life collects itself
around you. wind and sun.
mood. womb. face.
We will have been
neither happy nor sad
like a mother
with no hands
collecting life
around you.

THE DOOR OF THIS

The door of this castle is prayer.
—TERESA OF ÁVILA
The Interior Castle (1588)

Between here and somewhere
        lies a lopsided disjunctive bar
        a set-up for a supreme deviation
from life and its sumptuous interface

An atmospheric clouding denotes
        a subliminal lingual domination
        burning the toads
of cognitive dissonance in the face of death

Watering, wanting to grow the terrain
        consubstantial visions, a story of water
        plastic passions and sunken skulls
in the shadow's light, as an alternative

To repurpose our being (here)
        a euphoric solitude with a palate
        for the infinite, days when voluntary delusion
in an artificial paradise will have seemed just fine

Called, calling
        the innermost monitor
        a reciprocal sense of self
to other spaces we inhabit

In the moments prior to a sheath
        a layer, a shroud, never a wholesale merger
        settles into irreconcilable sediment
at the bottom it is always difference

At odds with what will have been
        or become
        submerged
in a connective medium

Vibration partitioned by stretches of gauze
        each abode also a node
        the soul enters within
itself, enfolds

Vacuoles, empty cells, porous spaces
        sheer husks lined by translucent skins
        still, we catapult
towards something

Encapsulated in catacombs
        the sinew of dream
        voids
held by an infinite net of night

VESSELS

Between Two Worlds

The magnetic pull of a cranium overcome
by fever, a drilling crater, an eruption

drip   drip   a   slow   leak

icicles;
prisms in heat

winter's strobe light

stalagmites

quiver by quiver

(pulsation)

Our heads heavy
when tipped on their sides

repeat to form an orbital ring around the night

walls grow
wings, hair, teeth
in wild wanting
to backpedal

Nighttime is for forgetting
                    for mending
                    for pretending

Repetition is one way to form an orbital ring around an object

Consonants and continents
freeze over then break
forming delicate husks

alcoves, pods
rental vessels
where we spend a winter
where we take up
a foreign language

a darkness
a smooth sheath
a winter's lake
nightfall
falls in
orbits

Slow seeps in the day

dawn's primal ribbons of rose, a shattering glare
blinding radiance

It's like we never even caught a wink

PLEASING THE VOID

In dream voids, the primordial
persona inhabits
alterity.

A singularity and a heavy door.

Partitions and spacing
walls and their painting
sea foam. forming.

The colour of ocean enlivens
personal space
the whoing and the whating
of the please at the core
of our being.

Swimming against
the morphology of desire
upholding cellular intelligence
the persistence of personhood
inundated
by dissolving.

Fragility
the key to disappearing.

You will have helped me so much
by repainting, tinting
the walls of a new dwelling
sea foam.

LOVE MAP OF THE AUDITORIUM

Why cannot the Ear be closed to its own destruction?

—WILLIAM BLAKE
The Book of Thel (ca. 1789)

A Lullaby

I.

We want watermelon
or at the very least its colour
to shine from our third eye
crying because we're babies
and we want what we want

Waxen forsythia and goldenrod line the passage
of this inner corridor

Sleep is what we drink to remember

A rivulet runs in the gutter

Flesh out of the mud reassembles
recollects

In audible fragments
carefully curated devotionals say for us
what our tongues are too tired to

Resorting to plaid for cover
an altruism that reeks of relapse
makes our hearing healing whole again

Repetition is one way to form an orbital ring around an object

Charged with a momentary lapse in amnesia
a short-term nexus of nepenthes, excuses
for a forget, for a dull fullness

In the gaps
the lacunae
left by your departure
a rapture sorts itself out

It's too late now for a lullaby to reach the inroads

Sleep is what we drink to remember

II.

Your song rests
on the outer helix
the prominent rim of the auricle
a winged fin

On the inside,
where it counts
invisible trails carve
into a cranium
the deep recesses
where the fontanelle has solidified

Echolalia
in a schematic perfect pitch
a well-thought-out pinnation
echoes

In the bony labyrinth
of the cochlea
we make our way past the old vestibule
we get turned around and around
semicircular canals

Finally shoved
into where the ecstatic happens
the subterranean
stone-dark decadent pallor

We find balance
in an auditory chamber
converting sound pressure
into irreverent electrochemical impulses
in a stone cathedral
panelled with wooden shafts
to enhance the reverberations

It's springtime in the Maritimes
The forsythias are in bloom
A rivulet runs in the gutter
Flesh out of the mud reassembles recollects
Where sound takes shape is just like the inside
of a snail's spiralled shell

III.

This canal is common to all mammals
except those that lay eggs
rather than bear their young live
still, they find it in their hearts
to nurse their spawn

We wade through the guttural back channels to recover our traces

A rivulet runs in the gutter

trying to piece together sound waves

Repetition is one way to form an orbital ring around an object

Sleep is what we drink to remember

a mocking bird   a diamond ring   a looking glass   a horse and cart

Murmurations
cooed into our ears

When you got back
we were sound
asleep

((((((*The apparition of opalescence*))))))

((((((*Here now, here you go, I've brought you back the moon*))))))

PERIODICALLY: A PERIODIC TABLE REMODELLED

The iteration of a smooth and dangling question
unable to fit into a too-tight box of no-hows.
Because of this I am stranded, shattered, simplified, and lost-taken.
Out of context it may seem as simple as a please
or a fainting-pretend
as simple as a six-sided snowflake pretending to be bird.
The listening eyes of an oak, the heart-rock of tinder
tenders the okay and then beams a combustible, universal YES!
The maybe-not-now that we'll never have been
no more a next-time permutation, a periodic movement
towards an element much denser, more noble. Truth
a compound too delicate to breathe between its pores.
What it may become next will be what it will have been
what it was once before. Beforehand
you stand a chance to behold and roll out
in re-emergence on reams of paper stacked to the brim-clouds.

Regard all things as a dream

Like the dialectics of a forest playing out in the memory of trees:

We all began here (in the forest)
became dis-located (somehow)
and returned (in the end)
to our roots

Like the way the moon does
when it sits on the topmost branch
of one of those one-thousand-year-old redwoods

withholding (doing nothing)

like that

IMPRINT

Tu ne sais ni où tu vas ni pourquoi tu vas,
entre partout, réponds à tout.

—ARTHUR RIMBAUD
"Mauvais sang,"
Une saison en enfer (1873)

Enter anywhere.
Be diaphanous.
Make soft your shape.
cat. cow. cobbler. shell.
Let the softness
the inkiness of you
settle in in the intaglio, seep
like walnut
oil into carved copper
ridges of line and form.

Leave an impression.
Leave an imprint
a mark of your body.
Be heavy enough.
Be here enough.
Decide
on something
then make it
soft, translucent.

Become a feather and float.
Become a winter moon and shimmer.
Become iridescent as amaranth.

Give a blood curdling balk – go ahead, wake them!

Now imagine sunlight glittering on the snow.
Now imagine sunlight dizzily drinking an open field.
Now imagine a wooded creek encircled
by a thousand shapes of death, shades
of the lily-livered that lay dormant within us, now departed
so that we may recoup
so that we may regain our ruddiness and footholds
in rebirth.

Learning
to bear the radiance
of it all.

Every swollen ego and effective trust.
Every malevolent gold digger and Mary Magdalene.
Every last revolver and open heart.

Is it possible
that rage be distilled enough
to be abandoned?

Just checking
because it's Pisces season
and the light of the crepuscule is mutable.

These signs are minuscule
but please, read them carefully.

Hold on to the banisters.
Something is shifting.

CITIES

An Intersubjective Ode to New Beginnings

I don't know anyone else here, but I like you
in the way that inner-city simultaneity
pushes up against the uncanny
unravelling of streets
that defy signifiers of liking
back alleys of appetitive yearning
urban encounters with meaning.

In the concavities
our nighttimes sprawl
in infinite nets
to the outskirts, winding the curvilinear quiver of edges.
dreaming. suburbia. eyelids. flutter.

This is what it looks like when you're sleeping.

Seeping into the psyche of a new city
marmoreal deities, medieval cathedrals
the partial ruins of our inklings
leanings we will have had about liking
confirmed by unknown urban planning
undergrounds and railings
park benches and places of public bathing.

In an atmospheric pressure
drop, we get to know the glisten
of wet asphalt
and get a coffee
to duck the rain
and the wind
and our faces
quiver a touch.

Tipping
we fumble with the change
of a foreign currency
still new to this city
of ourselves.

BEFORE SPEAKING

In the beginning
it switches our language.
A germinal rewiring of psyche sprouts
in the form of questions.
vivacious. soothing.
Where do the trees go when they grow legs and walk away?
In a way, you say, *that's so punk of them.*
I see what you are meaning to say. Switching
the primal fabric of our dreaming
a predisposition for thinking
we get up and go, furthering
the limbic traces of the ways we are changing
and the how of what we are meaning
when we say "going." ego thriving.
A panacea for the indeterminate going
of leaving language behind.
A language we're switching, sprouting
at the juncture of where we can agree
on meaning. moon and stars.
At a distance the sensorium is communicating, gently
caressing the creases of staying.
switching. vivacity. night. moon. stars.
We're learning to communicate
in the dream language of traces
we will have been leaving.
In the beginning, before speaking.

WHAT WE KNOW WE KNOW

I. WHAT WE KNOW

Walking into the face of a mountain
blue, like my skin and you
see me only from behind
counting backwards in units of intensity
seeking psychic legitimacy as revelation.
In the dream you never see my face. knowing.
What we know is what is knowable. intelligible.
Becoming
also a way of saying
beauty. creases. soft shell. belly. face.
mountain. facing. effacing.
folds and faults.
lines. intensities. A rapture
enfolded in becoming.
The soft places where you feel nice.
amethyst and lavender.
The rapture of who I am
becoming. beauty. knowing.
It will turn you on a bit
and you will not have known
what to make of it at first.

II. WHAT WE DO NOT KNOW

A future time in which I am part-time you
and you are also part-time me.
A future in which there will have been a fire
it will consume.
What we don't know is unknown. unknowable.
What we don't know we don't know.
What to make of this future fire?
We cannot be accountable
for an enfolded tense. Fire
it will consume
intelligibility. possessions.
books. a house.

It will turn you on a bit.
You will become possessed.
The fire will make us grow
uncomfortably close
in intensities
for the time being, opacity.
We will not have been able to know
in advance how at home we would be
in one another.
It's hot that you want to read me
Baudelaire in the bath.
I'm at once enflamed and submerged
by the idea.

SEA CHANGE

A found poem, it will have been read again after all this time

I.

striped
shell shucks
cordage

process of taking apart
break   in
smoothness
evenness of surface
low continuous beating of drum
playfulness
disintegration
of rocks
outer covering
   of oyster
   or clam
high-pitched
twining collectively of ropes

II.

wink
inflections
diapason knells
scrolls of silver snowy sentences
sceptred terror
sessions
stars
Adagios of islands
Prodigal
turning shoulders
sleep, death, desire
flower
vortex

movement of
wave coming
up and closing
down on beach
rich medieval
  fabric
each wave is
a scroll on which
there is written your
death sentence

full range
        of music
                death
authority
        courtroom
                justice
                        legality

movement, seasons
          saviour
    colour imagery
music motif   lover
    form wave
    still point
     incircle
waves move   round   flower
   looking
& seeing becomes
          more & more
    important

encounter
rendered in
terms of natural
elements of sea & sky

III.

ribboned water
wave on wave unto
Your body

blood relationship
brings
forth, carry
washed
small box for keeping, exhibiting relic
flexible triangular shape

rapport & harmony of nature
spiritual nature
symbolic preservation of experience
of love

IV.

I know as spectrum
                    gulf on gulf
Whose circles bridge, I know
clay
fatal tides
resign
Blue latitudes

sea –
symbol of
timelessness
body of flesh
physical love
undeniable – indestructible
contort – encircle
                        death in water
                        done over &
                        over again
wreath –
   twine
      together

part of
church for clergy
embodied in human flesh
      – absolute, ideal
"*consanguinity*"

oar
over Mars
Venus
under *petals*

flower
imagery

v.

estuaries
hard sky limits
remembered stars
What words
moonlight
cleft of sky
slant of drifting foam
Your breath sealed by the ghosts I do not know

sharpness
  severed
rough   white icy
      covering
      from fog
   cannot
be   broken
bridge
pediment turned
   upside down
cleavage   imagery – divinity
voyage privacy
naval cable
despair
   or
call to
  surrender
don't
fight
time
accept time

sleep the long way home

VI.

lost morning eyes
under stranger skies
shell secretes
O rivers mingling
still fervid covenant
hair
imaged Word

wreathing
hard
outer
covering
or boat
separate substance
and eliminate

immortality
rebirth

something

wild
disordered

one floating flower

petalled word

“birth
  of
Venus”
goddess
    of love
brightest
planet
mysterious

never
      ending

way in which
   we experience the absolute

the eternal reply
never   permanent   *farewell*

WE'VE BEEN DREAMING THIS FOR EONS

In search of clarity
a definitive all-caps nope is preferable
to the conceptual form of you
the you that goes to bed as a one
and then wakes up more as a zero
that you, but in reverse
more absence than presence.

In your dreams you're you
but the B-side.

Encoded in a forest
there's an embedded lake
sometimes
you bring me to the edge and then
walk away

I fall in.

Like rain that comes just before disappearing
into the woods, it's case by case.
Every forest is its own thing.
Every forest does its own thinking
sometimes splitting its trees
like wishbones or tuning forks.

It feels like the splitting is an okay thing
because we have the feeling that it is
and then, when we don't
it isn't.

Overnight, encased by nightfall
the trees and lake bear witness
to an ancient dream and a mass grave.

I am only one mirror, you say, *and the middle of the lake*
is a different point of view.

This, I say, *is what happens when you don't pay attention*
to your unconscious.

When you speak you have something
that resembles a lisp but isn't
an impediment
something like knotted sinew webbing
laced across the oracular caverns
of your oral history

it sometimes catches dreams.

Filtering the inverse of necessity
you find yourself in nothing but a sometimes
mirrored lake reflecting
light and trees.

I come back to bed in the mornings to dream in your dreams
sometimes I'm still dreaming you and you are
sometimes still dreaming me

but in reverse.

light. lake. trees. memory. rain.

Repetition
is another way of forming
an orbital ring around an object.

I am a lake in the middle of a forest
doing my own thing
thinking
about your mirrored presence

Then, like light
I will have disappeared in the trees.

A CLOUD OF

The nature of love is such that it shares everything.

—ANONYMOUS

The Cloud of Unknowing

(late fourteenth century)

The alchemy of a cloud
of unknowing

lodged between you
and your darkest sequence

an algorithm
of more or less

of the beyond
of what I am

and what you are
becoming

A luminous refraction
a catalogue

evaporates our former selves'
surface mist

at the spacing between
intervals

coffee and cigarettes
wanting, waiting

for this maternal inking
to pass

Regenerating cells ad infinitum
on a plausible arc

of becoming
our finitude
will have amounted, mostly

to no more no less
than the sum total

of what we imagine
beneath a cloud of forgetting

to be more real
than our mouths and hands

I am of two minds

PARTIAL ECLIPSE REPLICA STILLS

Still here
coasting the remarkable.

We will have fathomed somehow
a shiv to the lunar.

eclipse. fathom. darkness. somehow. memory. rain.

Shedding this heart husk
growing
into the next to channel
electro-animal magnetism
and still possible shadows
and wavelengths that say
Let's do this!

Let's throw around dark matter
watch it flicker and move to sound.

morning. traffic. rain.

You've got it all backwards, my dear
it's not repression of desire that causes anxiety
it's the other way around.

Let's call instinct video art.

sublimate. darkness. memory.

Pixels brush up against skin
correlating to nothing but
the libidinal tipping point
between submission
and domination played out
projected on skin
as screen for the pleasure of repetition.

repetition. eternal. fathom. skin. night. memory. darkness. rain.

Still,
the light matters
making the most of this
flailing hollow throb
pulsating photosynthetic attraction.

light. memory. instinct. moon. rain. fathom. eternal. still.

Without the love of your pixels I am nothing.

Moreover, still
every now and again

I microdose you
on the Blood or Harvest or Sturgeon Moon.

O'KEEFFE IN THE FLESH

You will have wanted so much to say
Oh Apple, I love you, I love you!
as she shifts the air with her hand
self-organizing
realizing for the first time
how upsetting the flesh tones are
reminiscent of the queasy smell of glue
a macabre aromatherapy.

A smooth, elegant
if not effeminate contrapposto
of a skull, pelvis, and sometimes
antlers leaning into fleshy landscape.

The depth perception of clouds
mountains. leaves. flowers. driftwood.
beg for a savage salvation out
of here to a beyond much softer
even than these pastel creases
and libidinal folds.

Then there are the times when
the subconscious spews up a little
oracular revelation:
When it eventually happens
I'll want it to be more
like I've swallowed a watermelon
and not become
as big and beautiful as a house
or anything that would stretch

my middle out of shape
or tie me down to a discourse
reserved for talking about
the changing forms of bodies
or the amorphous
malleable nature of skin
stretched like oil on canvas
in broad strokes.

In the case of absence
memory coasts our heart-minds.

We cleave to a shoreline
a sublime horizon
in search of
new things to think
new things to say
new things to keep
to ourselves.

A variety of possible endings.

A CASE OF DISPLACED UTERUS

The exoskeleton of a crab glistens on butterscotch
pebbles smoothed
over by waves and ocean wants

Giving up an agenda of taming
          a wandering animal

        Not even the fronds of witch hazel
nor the thallus of deadly nightshades
      can account for the
                    migration
          of a womb

And to think … A living thing living inside another living thing!

They collude in poisonous rumours
        about her
          bewildering
hormonal state

Scoop is she's got the morbs

An overgrown garden!

Rampant belladonna!

The migratory hysteria
          of a displaced uterus

defiantly wanders the anima's hollows
vacillating through passageways and vacancies of a vacant

body

Mystifying

constricting vitals
obstructing breath
causing disease

conjuring

illness
as metaphor

Wreaking havoc!

One sky stacked upon
another neatly This is how
it should be nothing out of
bounds All phenomena in
their rightful places layered
and/or tucked tucked
modestly between two flanks

Unclot and decompress by spasm

How simple
a cure

Seaside vapours:
Salt, a twinge of pine

The squall of seagulls, condensation
of water in the air

Revitalizing!

Simply a fantastic ...

scientific conundrum as inexplicable

as a cranberry sky turned ready-made

A diagnostic

Clearly
something is not right

Something is not in place

The sky is having her moontime

Oh no! Not again!

ALMOST EQUIVALENTS

Clouds were there for everyone ... If the cloud series are
due to my powers of hypnotism I plead "Guilty."

—ALFRED STIEGLITZ
letter, September 19, 1923

I. GO / NO-GO ZONE

This atmosphere is so patchwork right now
so all over the place, so neither here
nor there, I can't even
begin to tell you.

All touch and go
in the go / no-go zone. Either
a very cunning boy or a truly rubber girl.
What will it take?

A rose-quartz vortex tincture?
Do I need to wear a tie-dyed turban and
woo-woo poncho just to convince you
I've seen the light

poking through the bulbous cumulus
clouds stretching out for a moment
of sustained attention in the jejune July sky
tinted popsicle in ambivalence?

Just saying. It's fabulous.
Next time I'll be better prepared.
Next time I'll try harder.

Next time I'll try for Paris, maybe
and hold the Eiffel Tower within purview
at all times. Or maybe not
drift so far downstream and stay

closer to home instead. The Adirondacks.
Next time it will not have been so scattershot.
Next time I will have had an umbrella.

II. BOUNDARY CONDITIONS

Maybe after all
I *am too* a waterfall
with a bunch of rogue lipids
gathering round the bend
to keep the H_2O out

a boundary attempt
at the molecular level.
Nature's little way of saying
These are not real waterfalls, fellas!
A prism. The shutter recasting
the allure of (unmentionables)
in the best possible light.

Pitched in the right halogen glare
this indefinite monochrome
not-knowing cloud could
almost be seen as a good thing.

Like, how we now wear conflicting
layers of denim with irony
blue-jean gestures
to a stonewashed era gone by.

As a compendium to our wardrobe
a river runs through us.
We're also estuaries, you know
with simple vows. renew.

Tell me again that story
about the time when I undressed
how it gave off distortion
and a bleeping rainbow.

Tell me again
what a river I am
and how you wish
you could point your aperture

both at me and the sky
at the same time
in double exposure
running between
your gelatin banks.

Tell me again how much
I'm your one and only
true silver waterfall.

Oh yeah, and by the way, remind me
just who, exactly, is testing your reality-testing mechanism?

BIRTH OF VENUS

Offshoots of flammable kindness
give shape to a pliable oceanic bile.
A moondial turning, renovating humanism
as Venus straddles the world.
A giving. A plenum
in which auxiliary meditations
count for nothing more than
breath breathing itself
into life. Shape
by shape, counting. Fanning
the flame of making.
plying. Supplying
form as a medium for pleading.

Applying
no-longer-applicable shapes
to the bending as a prelude
to the deluge of taking.
A noble shellac shelling
overhangs the parallax of birthing.

Emerging from waves and ocean
wants, wanting nothing. Arriving
fully formed. Shaped
by the making of eros swooping
in in formidable subjugation.
Now, just because it's time, love,
doesn't mean that we will. You see
the shape we are taking
is a giving, an invocation
of the shapes we will be

making in the future form of partaking
a meditation on the shapes
we will have made by pleading.
bending. remodelling. sharing.

breathing. Breath
mistaken for Beauty's
pliable flaming.

LANDSCAPE MALFUNCTION

sunsets on the prairies are long over

done is the fog's quiet dance socking in the persimmon skyline

a fine pelt   a residue   an eager mist

on what used to be

a   h   o   r   i   z   o   n

a decisive line between ocean and sky

blurred now into a realm of abstraction devoid of the sublime

in a state

of more or less

HELIOTROPE

Like the intricate herringbone
of ascending and descending stairs

a current
going both ways

every so often
an archway

a natural pause.

Taking in the heliotrope
through spokes of dawn

we enter
the reticular formation

in the depths of our skulls
the impatiens bloom.

In the impulsivity of graphite
in the margins
in the interval

between *The Ravishing
of Lol Stein* and *Summer Rain*

we loot the pistachio-grey
dulse-strung
South Shore
for driftwood
and the exoskeletons of crabs

filling our pockets
the sky begins to bulge.

Subjective truth
being off-season
our altered egos
will have broken
most of the rules
groping for innocence
without mythos.

DWELLING PATTERN

Our house will have had
a basement, an attic
and two floors pleated
into an upper and a lower.

We'll have woven in
a lace-trimmed lattice
and taffeta windows
left open
to an enfolded infinity,
we'll have forged ourselves
in gnathic certainty,
that is to say, scissor
ourselves
a way to let out a little
at the seams and at the same time
let in the snakes
of deep-seated regret
(the time you wish you had
stayed but couldn't, the time you wish
you left but didn't know how)
the serpentine darkness
of underground abdominal
cavities, a gnawing
feeling that tells us
how to find a way
out of our dwelling patterns.

Our hemmed-in sages
suggest we install sequins
a skylight even
and gorge ourselves
on ribboned iridescence
a little more radiance
than we can handle,
a cluster of moths' wings

and seashells, urging us
to reinhabit our organic hollows
those ensorcelled pockets
lined with velour, soft interiors
where we can sometimes be
ourselves
like pickerel and cutthroat trout
swimming through ribbons of eelgrass
as if

there were
no windows
no rain
and not a stitch
of tomorrow.

REORIENTING

What if we let the seams show
a little when we breathe

What if when we breathe
we let a little tenderness
toughened by hindsight
tip the topography of inner
landscapes, reorienting
our grounding to pleasure

What if when we breathe
we use the floor
to overcome dogma
i.e., confined spaces
and push up against
the compactness
of seams that insist
on adjacencies
and junctures

What if we are breathing in
hindsight the "what if"
of the problematic of pleasure
as that which we will have been
willing to weather

Reorienting
to the terrain at hand
proposes breath as a medium

dissolving the seams; letting
out a little

in retrospect

FLOOR PLANS FOR INFINITY

You are in bloom. Blooming
into the places that make you see
the god of your understanding
hallucinating an asymmetric
seismic mystery
cherry pink and apple blossom white.
Enmeshed in conversation with the sky
and deities of your devising
a conversion process
of mattering, mind-altering.
mouthing. lip-synching. glossing.
concentric circles. Holistic
mystical entering
elaborated on linoleum flooring
before we knew each other by name
giving meaning
before leaving.
dark matter. cherries. velour.
An attempt at knotting.
Floored, we can't make out
what's happening.
dilating. concentric circles.

A tautology encircling
the blooming.

Besides, you had a flight to catch
in the morning.

IN OTHER WORDS: AN EXQUISITE CORPSE

The incandescence of reflective glass
gives you away
to a holographic horizon

to what it means to be seen
as two things at once

Shredding our stories
to ribbons
will more likely have been the way
we arrived at the belated epiphany:

That's us!
That is the proportion in (t)here!

When looked at in terms of
erosion, collision, explosion
(in other words: shipwreck, train wreck)

the flotation of a structure
(in other words: house, abode)

suggests the layout of an abstraction
bisected into bits prompting at once
the feeling of being
at home and displaced

A sprawling cluster of composites
onion-layered one upon the other
(in other words: an exquisite corpse)

The structure you find yourself in
in respite, a safe space
to lunch, say, is where you don't
have to see it. Within
is the only place
where it ceases to persist
along the excessive fluorescent skyline

Arguably, we could have ended it
(in other words: deciphered things differently)
by bending, but we both knew
and felt that it was the doing and
the saying and the thinking and the thinking
of the saying and the doing
of the thinking that accounted for
communication
a felt understanding
of the Platonic forms of afterlife

The cobalt hologram of an organism
and a floating floor
impregnate the desert
plains of Azerbaijan

A mirage

Suppose for a moment
that we didn't give up so easily
on where we want to be buried
in our life's work, that prized vantage point
of an inside where we understand each other's
hearts and sandstorms so fully

From the lofty belvedere on which we stand
careful Cupidian procedures
fill our radiant heartspace with the drone
of honeybees and a thousand glittering mirrors

The vision of our hearts
The nectar of inner beauty

(in other words: landscape, worldview, universal reception)

THIS SKY IS ALSO AN ENWRAPPED DELUSION

The way to conduct the clouds
is first to place them in columns
then let them clatter as they will
in looming torrents.

Seeing the syncopation for what it is:
a freestyle thunderstorm resolving itself
in quarter-tone clusters of dissonance
running three-quarters of a mile long.

The sky bulges over
finding clarity
in lateral dispersion
before it rains
or after it snows
or just then
when a bird flew over
the corrugated concrete
casting its shadow
for a flooded second.
The appeal of thunder.

A premonition:
A pair of twins, one wrapped
around each leg.
Together we clung to the sunset
and the sky yawned
keeping her mouth open
long enough to let in
a little more oxygen and suppress
the hardwiring of motherhood.

This may be why
it's only
the blue we see
registered as colour

in the scattering of light
the azure of sky
simply a synecdoche for irreverence
is its own kind of beauty
awkward
and tragic
and incomplete.

Under the collateral
of a scintillating desert night
getting ever colder
as the clusters of hydrogen
get more bright
the stars test their mettle
for the rapture
we've all been
waiting for.

It's a wonder
how they hold up against gravity
how ever did they get over it?

You've come too close now, they whisper,
we can't fall asleep in the same sleeping bag as you.

FROM THE OUTSIDE

We are creating a loophole
a visual palindrome
in which rain rains
on either side of a windowpane.
This is really you, you say again
I'm not sure I know what you mean.
We open all the windows and doors.
We place it outside by naming birds and trees.
pine-sparrow. walnut-lark. maple-pheasant.
birch-starling. *Holy Oak!*

Their shapes are pleasing
we are at ease
it's easy, it's exciting.
We can't explain what's happening.
I'm getting to know you, you're saying, *from the inside.*
Meanwhile, on the outside, we're naming.
This is really you, you say again.
We can't explain it, but it's what's happening.

We open all the windows and doors.
In the threshold, time frames the firmament
a site-specific shaping of what's outsiding
entering and exiting.
We will have been nesting
a reference to the love we make
when we mean to say falling.
feathers. branches.

A process of overriding
the insiding.

By way of naming, we are creating.
We put it outside, explaining the exciting.

Nestled, on the inside
a hologram of what we know
is happening.

A nebula of predicates ferments
the flip side
of naming.

FRUITING BODIES

this is a life preserve and a poem

a pseudo haiku filters
our nano-poetries
organizing epiphanies
along ogives we already know
offshore
will have been an oversimplified plan
to make this more porous
more livable
sustainability
shores up as shorthand
for utopia
preservation. preserving. marmalading.
you are the making of a poem
inside my body, fruiting
in autumnal blossoming

peeling orange skins
rose petal. water. clove. fall.
you poem inside

PERSIMMON

You will have caused it
to happen
in coefficient dreamtime multiplied
to the power of an illumined persimmon
and cranberry sunset

Fulfilling forgiveness as a skyline
embodying, embroidering
holding patterns caused by a lifetime
of regretting
an accidental act of tipping

A cross-stitched conditional
sense of self selfing the causal
causality causing the dream to happen

Freeing, unstitching the skyline
a capacity for forgiving what happened
while you were dreaming
serving as a segue
to illumination

Persimmon and cranberry
patterning pertains
to a capacious forgiveness
for the moments just before
the drowning

Giving cause to the causing
haunting. The sun
rising and setting
letting it happen
while dreaming

SEE-THROUGH

In an insomniac forest
she will have cut off all my hair
saying, *it unburies your face*

Until then I didn't know
I was so hidden
under dreams of one day
becoming
see-through

In the back of my mind
there are fears of drowning
in a bowl of wonton soup
or that housekeeping may check
the bedside-table drawers
fears both fabricated and plausible
swim against the current
of a suppressed urge
to climb into a loaf of bread
just to see what it would be like

Where there stands a chance
to uncouple your departure
from the world
with the wound
it left behind
there are still split ends
and holes left to dig
and holes left to fill
things to do
and wrinkles to make
around your eyes

Now, even the thought
of buttering toast
saddens my insides
confirming our hungers
are stale and aligned

REPARATIONS

There are many of us, here
in real time, realizing
for the first time
what an assemblage theory
of coexistence
might look like: porcelain sculptures
made of other, broken
porcelain sculptures reconfigured
to form *something that is awkward*
and a little bit tragic
but also incomplete.

Reparations: The real
fragility
a repatriation of our fissures
our fragile estrangement
from one another.

The dividends
of our brokenness
repurposed
after so many
incarnations
in these heady times
of realization, repair work
will be needed.

IT'S HEALING TO KNOW

The trees are breathing me
better

Taking and sending

The universe filtered in reverse
osmosis is how I'll keep giving
the world back to itself

It's healing to know
I had you confused
with someone else
It's healing to know
you were confused too

Breathing in
dark sound shadows that make my throat hurt

Breathing out
cool moonlight on a river lined by trees

the soft rustle of their leaves
breathing me
better

EVENTIDE

The moon flower opens at eventide.
A hedonic dulcimer drone accompanies
the secretions of a honeycomb, a semi-precious
stand-in for love conflated
with domesticity. Grief
grieves what is grievable.

Compartmentalized in the hiving
of memory. hexagonal devising. revising.
pollinating. quiver by quiver. Combing over
combining a past into the future
overcoming vectors, cross-pollinating
the future with the past.

It will have taken will to power our hivings.
body memory. earth memory. water memory.
Even the moon overflows sometimes
showing us the eternal parts of ourselves
in golden somatic opening
flowering domestic quivers
in the eventide.
The ever-present internalized.
hiving. flowing. overcoming.

LIGHT WAVES THE LEAVES

I will have seen the words
coming out of your eyes
on waves of light. Wavelengths
of your thought processes undulating.
In link for a moment we are submerged
under water, surrounded by glistening silver
fish penetrating the light waves emanating
from the aggregates of thought
in your eyes.

In your eyes
an effervescence, a wavelike thinking
moving thought through you. The wind
makes the light wave and I like it.
I'm sensing, I'm seeing
your thinking, like the watery
movement of liking
the light between the leaves moving
scintillating in the breeze. We're linking
liking. leaves. light. memory. waves.

A CABIN IN THE WOODS

Larkspurs heralding
a beginning, like air filling
a building. Budding
our spring hearts soonly to be being
an almost awakening
a springtime being
of hearts soon to be finding
a near future
perfect erasure
erasing shadows' darks.

Lip-synching, sidestepping
feeling for the contours of an unknown
beginning
in a cabin in the woods.

Breath filling, lips mapping
a making of shadows' sideways taking
sidestepping a near future
erasing shadows' darks.
Discovering each other in hiding.
A cabin in the woods as time in the making
a refuge to our liking.

Letting it in
we are awakening
in the wake of making
the synchronic meaning
of building.
branches. larkspurs. branching.
Budding hearts
erasing the darks.
Sidestepping the shadows
cast by a fire

you are building
you add another log
to the wood stove
replacing what we will have been
truly feeling.

Soonly, soonly
a slow-to-be springtime
becoming, beginning
in a cabin in the woods
in which we wear nothing
but antlers and black lace
where we can be our selves
where we potentiate our slightly
tantric shadows

where we open
all the windows
and let in the rain
and the wind
and the one who has no face.

TREE LINE

Along the cliffs
and crags
folds and faults
we gather our complicit parts
moving headlong into the rock face
edging ever closer to meaning

We scale the flank, lip, and shoulder
of this dark passage
at the brink of breath

Shouldering the howling
holy holy holy
holy holy holy holy

We will have made it
past the landslip and above
the leafiest of treelines

This lovely rarefied air
makes it hard to breathe
but in it we are so alive

cedared to the rafters
oaked to oblivion
spruced to the brim

Branching ever skyward in an arborization of words

REFERENCES AND INSPIRATIONS

GENE LOSS

a guide for the perplexed: a nod to Maimonides's *The Guide for the Perplexed* (ca. 1190).

AFTER YOU WENT NOVA

Seeing from the inside: based on Thích Nhất Hạnh's *Five Steps to Mindfulness* (2020) as interpreted by Ken McLeod (see Unfettered Mind, online).

A POEM ABOUT A DREAM ABOUT A MAN WHO DRANK TEA, HAD LOOSE IDEAS ABOUT GRAVITY, AND DIED TRYING TO TRANSVERSE THE SEVEN BRIDGES OF KÖNIGSBERG BY FALLING DOWN AN ELEVATOR SHAFT

The poem is an ode to the Hebrew song "Kol Ha'Olam Kulo" (The whole entire world) by Rabbi Baruch Chait, adapted from an epigram accredited to the Hasidic Rabbi Nachman of Breslov (1772–1810):

כָּל הָעוֹלָם כֻּלּוֹ	**Kol Ha'Olam Kulo**
כָּל הָעוֹלָם כֻּלּוֹ גֶּשֶׁר צַר מְאֹד וְהָעִקָּר לֹא לְפַחֵד כְּלָל.	The whole world is a very narrow bridge, and the main thing is not to fear at all.

all possible worlds: on "the best of all possible worlds," see Gottfried Wilhelm Leibniz's *Théodicée* (or *Essays of Theodicy on the Goodness of God, the Freedom of Man and the Origin of Evil*, 1710).

HELLO, WORLD!

"*hello, world!*" used to illustrate the basic syntax of computer programming languages.

THE DOOR OF THIS

disjunctive bar: see Jean-François Lyotard's *Libidinal Economy* (1974).

in the shadow's light: see Yves Bonnefoy's 1991 book of the same name.

in an artificial paradise: see Charles Baudelaire's *Les Paradis artificiels* (*Artificial Paradises*, 1860).

the soul enters within / itself: from Teresa of Ávila's *The Interior Castle* (1588).

VESSELS

Between Two Worlds: The poem's subtitle is after S. Ansky's play *The Dybbuk*, or *Between Two Worlds*, written between 1913 and 1916 and first performed in 1920 by the Vilna Troupe in Warsaw.

dawn's primal ribbons of rose: inspired by Homer's figurations of Dawn in the *Odyssey*.

LOVE MAP OF THE AUDITORIUM

Sleep is what we drink to remember: found text, from a graffiti, artist unknown.

a mocking bird a diamond ring a looking glass a horse and cart: from the traditional Southern United States lullaby "Hush, Little Baby."

PERIODICALLY: A PERIODIC TABLE REMODELLED

Regard all things as a dream: a Buddhist aphorism, part of Tonglen practice.

the dialectics of a forest: after Gaston Bachelard's *The Poetics of Space* (1958).

IMPRINT

Enter anywhere and opening quote from Arthur Rimbaud's "Bad Blood," in *A Season in Hell* (1873): "You do not know where you are going, nor why you are going; enter anywhere, reply to anything."

WHAT WE KNOW WE KNOW

On *intensity* and *intensities*, see Gilles Deleuze and Félix Guattari's *A Thousand Plateaus: Capitalism and Schizophrenia* (1980).

SEA CHANGE

Found poem compiled from the marginalia and underlined passages of Hart Crane's "Voyages," as found in a vintage copy of *The Complete Poems of Hart Crane* (1958).

PARTIAL ECLIPSE REPLICA STILLS

It's not repression of desire that causes anxiety: inspired by Anne Carson's *Eros the Bittersweet* (1986).

A CASE OF DISPLACED UTERUS

illness as metaphor: after Susan Sontag's book of the same name (1978).

A living thing living inside another living thing!: The "wandering womb" was a belief held in ancient Greek medicine that a woman's womb, sometimes in itself depicted as an "animal," would become dislodged and wander around her body, causing bouts of suffocation and "hysteria" (from the Greek *hustera* ὑστέρα, "womb"). Second-century medical writer Aretaeus of Cappadocia's figuration of the womb is of "a living thing inside another living thing." Remedies besides marriage and childbearing included scent therapies and herbal concoctions.

ALMOST EQUIVALENTS

After Alfred Stieglitz's photographs of clouds in his series *Equivalents* (1925–1934). Epigraph found in Vicki Goldberg, *Photography in Print: Writings from 1816 to the Present* (UNM Press, 1988), where the following source is given: "From [a] letter written by Stieglitz 'With no idea of publication,' as printed in *The Amateur Photographer and Photography*, September 19, 1923; p. 255."

hold the Eiffel Tower within purview / at all times: after Roland Barthes's essay "The Eiffel Tower," in *The Eiffel Tower and Other Mythologies* (1979).

BIRTH OF VENUS

Inspired by Sandro Botticelli's *The Birth of Venus* (ca. 1484–1486). On *eros swooping*, see Anne Carson, *Eros the Bittersweet* (1986).

HELIOTROPE

The Ravishing of Lol Stein (1964) and *Summer Rain* (1990) are both novels by Marguerite Duras.

DWELLING PATTERN

pleats and *enfolded infinity* inspired by Gilles Deleuze's *The Fold: Leibniz and the Baroque* (2006).

FLOOR PLANS FOR INFINITY

cherry pink and apple blossom white: after the 1950 popular song "Cherry Pink and Apple Blossom White" ("Cerisier rose et pommier blanc") by Louiguy.

IN OTHER WORDS: AN EXQUISITE CORPSE

After the architecture of Zaha Hadid and Roland Barthes's essay "The Eiffel Tower," in *The Eiffel Tower and Other Mythologies* (1979).

That is the proportion: from Gertrude Stein's "The Life of Juan Gris / The Life and Death of Juan Gris," in *Portraits and Prayers* (1934).

to lunch, say, is where you don't / have to see it: after Roland Barthes's "The Eiffel Tower," in *The Eiffel Tower and Other Mythologies* (1979).

IT'S HEALING TO KNOW

Taking and sending: a meditation practice known as Tonglen and used in Tibetan Buddhist Lojong ("Mind Training") practice. See Buddhist meditation master Chekawa Yeshe Dorje's *Training the Mind in Seven Points*, one of the root texts in Lojong, as well as Ken McLeod, "Mind Training in Seven Points," Unfettered Mind, online.

EVENTIDE

grievable: after Judith Butler's *Frames of War: When Is Life Grievable?* (2010).

TREE LINE

holy holy holy / holy holy holy holy: after the Kaddish (קדיש), the Jewish mourner's prayer, and also a homage to Allen Ginsberg's 1955 "Footnote to Howl" (*Collected Poems, 1947–1980*, Harper & Row, 1984).

ACKNOWLEDGMENTS

With heartfelt gratitude ...

To my family and friends, both alive and departed, for sustaining me in my being, doing, making, and thinking processes ... and to the community of writers, both in my immediate circles and beyond, for creating a field of resonance. And to all those who generously read and offered encouraging feedback on early drafts along the way.

Many thanks to Talonbooks: to Les Smith for designing the cover; to Nicole Razia Fong and Charles Simard for their attentive reading and generative editorial insights. And a special thanks to Catriona Strang for holding communicative space for this project over *la longue durée* – across oceans and continents – helping this body of work take shape and evolve into fruition, and for editing with care.

I extend my appreciation to above/ground press and Broken Sleep Books. The poems "Imprint" and "We've Been Dreaming This for Eons" first appeared in *Dreamlands* (Broken Sleep Books, 2021).

Previous iterations of "Hello, World!," From the Outside," "Light Waves the Leaves," "Wintering," "A Cabin in the Woods," "Cities," "Eventide," "Before Speaking," "Birth of Venus," "O'Keeffe in the Flesh," "Reorienting to Pleasure," "It's Healing to Know," and "What We Know We Know" appeared in a different form in *Light Waves the Leaves* (above/ground press, 2020).

Thank you also to the journals, publications, and websites who featured earlier versions of some of the poems herein, and for including reviews of my previous work: *Contemporary Verse 2*; *ENTROPY*; anti*lang*; *Train: a poetry journal*; *periodicities: a journal of poetry and poetics*; *Poetry Pause* & *Fresh Voices* (by the *League of Canadian Poets*); *emerge*; *Sewer Lid*; *Bad Dog Mag*; *TERSE. Journal*; *Dovecote Magazine*; *Moonchild Magazine*; *Where Is The River*; and *FIVE:2:ONE* (*#thesideshow*).

In recognition of the support of the Canada Council for the Arts for a Research and Creation grant that enabled dedicated time for research and writing, as well as for time at the Writers Retreat at the Banff Centre for Arts and Creativity and in residency at the Fish Factory, Creative Centre of Stöðvarfjörður, Iceland.

RAZIELLE AIGEN is a poet and writer. Her poems, chapbooks, and interviews have appeared both in print and online across Canada, the United States, and the United Kingdom. She has taken part in writing residencies at several international art centres and is a recipient of a Research and Creation grant from the Canada Council for the Arts. *A Future Perfect* is Razielle's first book of poems.